A New True Book

WEATHER
EXPERIMENTS

By Vera Webster

This "true book" was prepared
under the direction of
Illa Podendorf,
formerly with the Laboratory School,
University of Chicago

CHILDRENS PRESS ®
CHICAGO

Earth from space

PHOTO CREDITS

National Aeronautics & Space Administration
(NASA) — 2, 38, 39

James P. Rowan — 4 (middle), 6 (bottom), 24

National Severe Storms Laboratory — 18 (bottom), 42

Lynn M. Stone — 4 (top), 14, 29 (right), 33

Margaret Thoma — 29 (left)

Tony Freeman — 4 (bottom)

Judy Potzler — 25

Reinhard Brucker — 6 (top), 41

Rich Havel — 6 (middle)

Joseph A. DiChello, Jr. — 10, 18 (top), 27

James M. Mejuto — Cover, 13 (2 photos), 20, 44

National Oceanic Atmospheric Administration
(NOAA) — 16 (top), 30 (2 photos), 35

Len Meents — 9, 11, 15, 16 (bottom), 22, 26, 28, 34, 37

Library of Congress Cataloging-in-Publication Data

Webster, Vera R.
  Weather Experiments.

  (A New true book)
  Includes index.
  Summary: Presents ten experiments involving heat,
wind, air, and water, which demonstrate how these
elements are related to weather.
  1. Weather—Experiments—Juvenile literature.
[1. Weather—Experiments. 2. Experiments.
I. Title. II. Series
QC981.3.W4318 1986   551.5'07'8   85-31425
ISBN 0-516-01662-8

TABLE OF CONTENTS

Weather Changes ... 5

Air and Weather ... 8

Heat and the Weather ... 10

Winds and the Weather ... 14

What Is Air?... 20

How Does Water Get into the Air?... 23

What Are Clouds?... 25

Where Does Snow Come From?... 31

What Is Air Pressure?... 33

Telling About the Weather ... 39

Things to Remember ... 43

Words You Should Know ... 46

Index ... 47

Rain clouds over
a marsh

Winter in Chicago, Illinois

Swimmers in California

WEATHER CHANGES

Weather changes. It changes from day to day. It changes from season to season. It is different in different parts of the world.

Saguaro cactus in Arizona

Palm trees in Nice, France

Snow in Rocky Mountains National Park

Where do you live?
Is it warm or cold there?
Is it sunny or cloudy?
Is it calm or windy?
Is it rainy or snowy?

AIR AND WEATHER

The Earth has land and water. It also has a layer of air around it.

You cannot see air. But you can see and feel what air can do.

Air is where the weather is. But it takes more than air to make weather.

EXPERIMENT

Take an empty glass.
Turn it upside down.
Then push it straight down into
a pan of water.
What happens?
No water enters the glass
because the glass is full of air.
Tilt the glass and the air will
pour out. Then water can go in.
Try it and see.

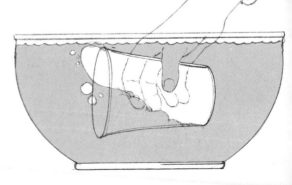

Sunrise

HEAT AND THE WEATHER

It takes heat to make weather. Heat from the sun warms the land and the water. The warm land and water warm the air.

EXPERIMENT

Hang two thermometers.
Hang one in the sunshine.
Hang the other in the shade.

Read the thermometer every hour. Write down the temperatures you read. Do this for two or three days.

Look at what temperatures you found. At what time of day was it warmest? When was it coldest?

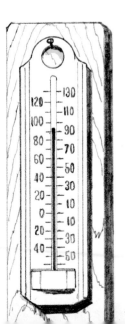

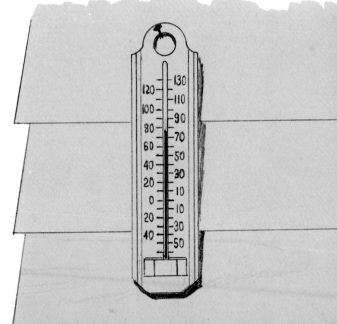

Fill two pans with dirt. Put the same amount of dirt in each pan.

Set one pan in the sunshine. Set the other in the shade. Let them alone for two hours.

Then take the temperature of the dirt in each pan. Are the temperatures the same? How are they different?

Fill two pans with water.

Set one pan in the sunshine. Put the other in the shade. Let them stand for two hours.

Then take the temperature of the water in the pans.

Is the temperature the same in each? How are they different?

Wind is moving air.

   Warm air rises. The
colder air moves
downward. This causes
winds. Winds are an
important part of our
weather.

Wind speed gauge

WINDS AND THE WEATHER

Air is always moving.
Wind is air that is moving
fast.

EXPERIMENT

Make a wind vane and see which way the wind is blowing.

Put a long pin through a spool.

Slip a drinking straw over the pin. The straw should be able to turn easily.

Glue a paper arrow to one end of the straw.

Put your wind vane outside.

Which way is the wind blowing?

Three-cup anemometer

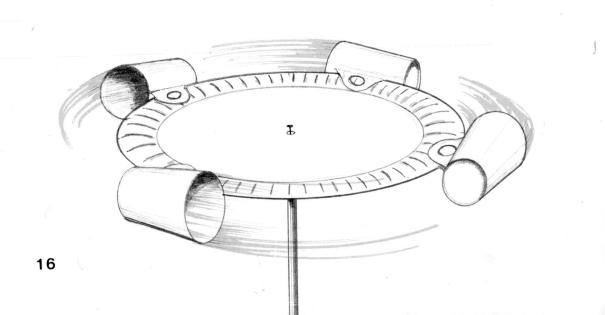

EXPERIMENT

You can make an anemometer and find out how fast the wind is blowing.

Take a paper plate. Staple the handles of four paper cups to the edge of the plate.

Put a long pin into the top of a thin stick or a long pencil.

Cut a hole in the paper plate. Slip the plate over the pin.

Put your anemometer in the wind.

How many times does it turn around in a minute?

Above: Helpful winds
dry clothes.
Right: This tornado
struck Union City,
Oklahoma on
May 24, 1973 and
caused great
damage.

Wind may be helpful. It can turn windmills. It can push sailboats through the water. It helps to dry clothes hanging on the line.

There are harmful winds. Tornadoes and hurricanes are very strong and dangerous winds.

Winter snows in Garrison, New York

WHAT IS AIR?

Air is made up of tiny particles. These are called molecules. Air molecules are too small to be seen. They bounce around a lot.

Air molecules move slowly when they are cool. They are close together when the air is cool. When the air is warm, the molecules move faster and farther apart. Then there is room for other things.

Dust floats around in the air then. Molecules of water are there also.

EXPERIMENT

Find two pans the same size. Put one-half inch of water in each.

Set one pan in the shade. Set the other in the sunshine. Look at them every day.

What happens?

The water in both pans disappears. But the water placed in the sunshine will probably disappear first.

HOW DOES WATER GET INTO THE AIR?

Heat makes molecules of water move faster and separate from one another. They move into the air. When this happens we say the water evaporates. Then we call it water vapor.

St. Croix River

Water evaporates from oceans, rivers, and lakes. It also comes from the ground and from plants. All air has some water vapor in it.

WHAT ARE CLOUDS?

Water vapor in the air forms clouds.

In clouds, water vapor has cooled. The molecules slow down and come together. Little drops of water form around bits of dust.

EXPERIMENT

You can make water vapor
form drops.

Fill a tin can with water and
ice.

Set the can over a bowl of
warm water.

Soon water vapor in the air
will form drops on the cold can.
The drops will run down the side
of the can.

Try it and see.

On some days, the
clouds look alike. Then the
rain comes down gently.
On other days, there are
black clouds. Then the rain
comes down hard. There can
be lightning and thunder
with this kind of storm.

EXPERIMENT

You can make a rain gauge
and find out how much rain falls.

Set an opened tin can in a
box of sand. Be sure it is
steady.

After the rain, measure the
water in the can.

How deep was the water?

Was it a half-inch, one inch, or
more?

Was it less than a half-inch?

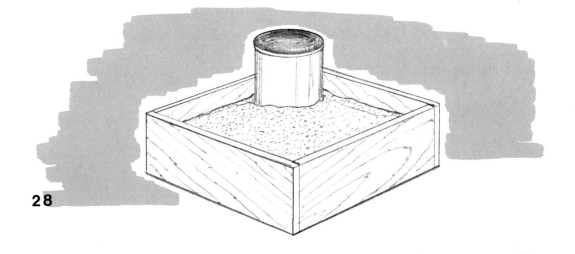

Fog can hide buildings and trees.

Sometimes clouds form close to the ground. Then we say it is foggy.

It is sometimes hard to see through the fog. So we must watch for cars when crossing the street. The drivers may not be able to see us.

WHERE DOES SNOW COME FROM?

Some days are cold enough for water to freeze. When the air is cold enough, water vapor in the air freezes before it can form drops of water. Then snowflakes form.

No two snowflakes are alike. But all snowflakes have six sides. These six-sided shapes are called crystals.

EXPERIMENT

Catch some snowflakes on dark-colored paper.

Look at the flakes through a magnifying glass.

You can see the crystals of ice.

Let your rain gauge fill with snow.

Then bring it inside. Let the snow melt.

What happens?

Your rain gauge is less than half full of water. But it was quite full of snow.

Snow has lots of air trapped in its crystals. When it melts, the air is freed.

Barometer

WHAT IS AIR PRESSURE?

Air pushes in all
directions. This push of air
is called pressure. Air
pressure is important to
weather.

33

EXPERIMENT

You can feel air pressure.
Get a plunger. Press it onto
the floor. Then try to pull it up.
What happens?
It is hard to pull it up. The air
was pushed out from the cup
when you pushed down. The air
outside the cup presses on the
cup. It holds it to the floor.

Temperature helps air pressure change. When the air is warm, its molecules are far apart. The air has little pressure. This is called a low. When air is cooler, it has more pressure. This is a high.

EXPERIMENT

A barometer can show changes in air pressure.

You can make a simple barometer.

Fasten a piece of a balloon over the top of a bottle with a rubber band.

Glue a drinking straw to the stretched balloon.

Glue a pin to the other end of the straw.

Make a chart. Put it behind your barometer.

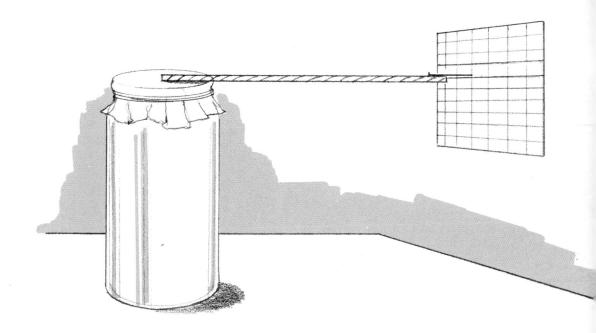

What happens?

Air pushes down on the stretched balloon. It makes the straw move when it changes. You can measure how it moves with your chart.

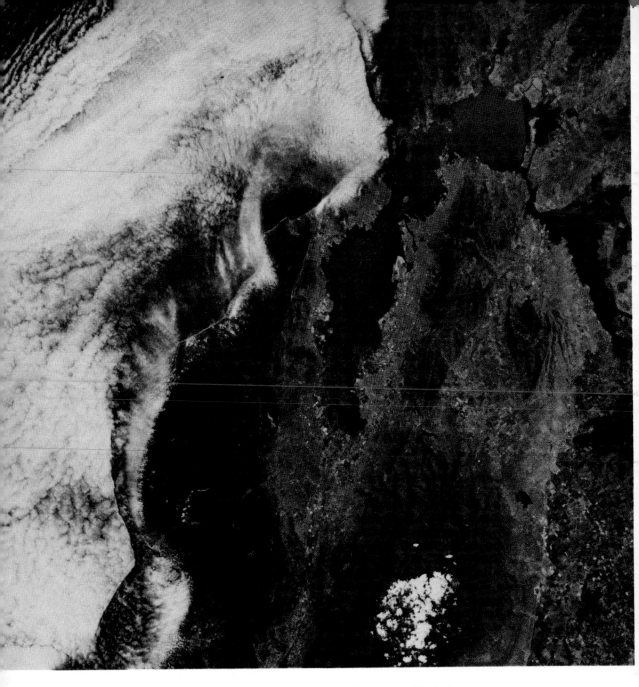

Photograph of San Francisco Bay in California taken from Skylab.
The Pacific Ocean is on the left.

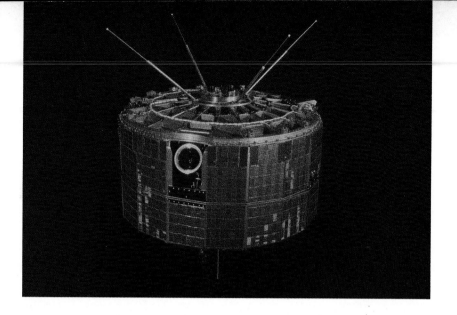

TELLING ABOUT THE WEATHER

Weather satellites go around the Earth. Their cameras take pictures of clouds, the land, ice in the sea, and hurricanes. Their instruments measure temperatures all over the world.

This information helps weather forecasters know about the weather. They keep track of these things:

- the temperature of the air
- the direction and speed of the wind
- the changing air pressure
- how much moisture is in the air
- the clouds
- how much rain falls

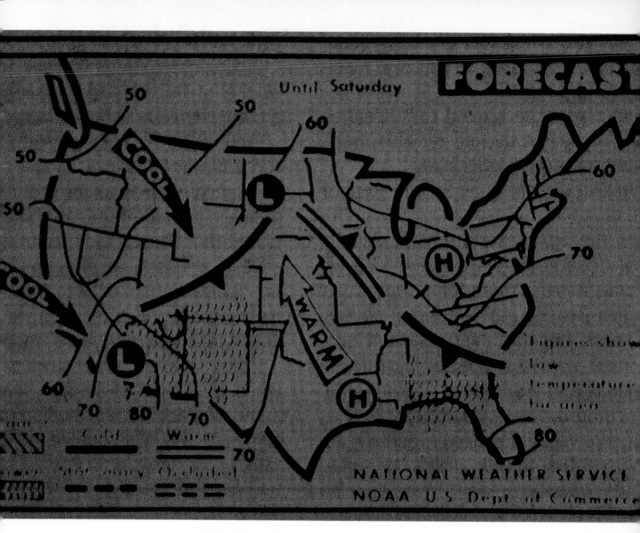

Weather maps are prepared by the National Weather Service.

Weather forecasters use this information to make weather maps.

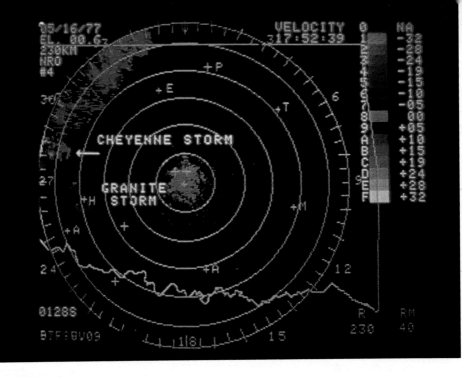

Radar screen showing tornado-like storms

Weather stations all over the world report to one large weather bureau. The weather bureau tells sailors on ships, airplane pilots, farmers, and other people about the weather.

THINGS TO REMEMBER

Weather occurs in the air. If there were no air, there would be no weather. Weather changes when the temperature changes. Changes in temperature cause wind. Changes in temperature change the air pressure. Weather is the result of heat, wind, pressure, and moisture.

Water evaporates to form water vapor. Water vapor condenses to form clouds and rain. When water vapor freezes before it forms rain, snowflakes form.

Weather is constantly changing. The sun is a great weather changer. Weather is important in our daily lives.

WORDS YOU SHOULD KNOW

anemometer(an • ih • MOM • ih • ter)—an instrument that measures speed of the wind

barometer(bah • ROM • ih • ter)—an instrument that measures the pressure of the atmosphere

calm(KAHM)—not windy; quiet

central(SEN • tril)—at or near the center; main

compare(kom • PAIR)—to say how things are the same or different

condense(kon • DENSE)—to change from a gas to a liquid

crystal(KRISS • til)—a solid substance with sides and angles that form a pattern

damage(DAM • ij)—to harm; injure

evaporate(ee • VAP • or • ate)—to change from a liquid to a gas

expand(x • PAND)—to get bigger

hurricane(HER • ih • kain)—a strong storm with very high winds and heavy rain

magnify(MAG • nih • fy)—to enlarge

molecule(MOL • ih • kyool)—the smallest part into which a substance can be divided and still be the same substance

orbit(OR • bit)—the path that objects in space take

particle(PAR • tih • kil)—a very small piece of something; speck

rain gauge(RANE GAYJE)—an instrument that measures the amount of rain that falls

satellite(SAT • ih • lite)—an object that moves in an orbit in space

surround(ser • ROUND)—to be on all sides of; encircle

thermometer(ther • MOM • ih • ter)—an instrument that measures temperature

tornado(tor • NAY • doh)—a very strong wind that whirls

wind vane(WIND VAIN)—an instrument that shows the direction of the wind

INDEX

air, 8, 9, 10, 13, 14, 20, 21, 23,
    24, 25, 31, 32, 33-37, 40, 43
air molecules, 20, 21, 35
air pressure, 33-37, 40, 43
anemometer, 17
changes in weather, 5, 45
clouds, 25, 27, 29, 39, 40, 45
crystals of snowflakes, 31, 32
dust, 21, 25
Earth, 8, 39
evaporation, 23, 24, 45
experiments:
  air, 9
  air pressure, 34, 36-37
  barometer, 36-37
  rain gauge, 28
  snow melting, 32
  temperature changes, 11, 12
  water evaporation, 22
  water vapor, 26
  wind direction, 15
  wind speed, 17
fog, 29
forecasters, weather, 40, 41
harmful winds, 19
heat, 10-12, 23, 43
helpful winds, 19
high (air pressure), 35
hurricanes, 19, 39
ice, 39

land, 8, 10, 39
lightning, 27
low (air pressure), 35
maps, weather, 41
moisture, 40, 43
molecules of air, 20, 21, 35
molecules of water, 21, 23, 25
rain, 27, 28, 40, 45
rain gauge, 28, 32
satellites, weather, 39
snow, 31, 32, 45
snowflakes, 31, 32, 45
sun, 10, 45
temperatures, 11, 12, 35, 39,
    40, 43
thunder, 27
tornadoes, 19
water, 8, 10, 21-26, 31, 45
water molecules, 21, 23, 25
water vapor, 23-26, 31, 45
weather bureau, 42
weather changes, 5, 45
weather forecasters, 40, 41
weather maps, 41
weather satellites, 39
weather stations, 42
wind, 13-19, 40, 43
wind direction, 15, 40
wind speed, 17, 40
wind vane, 15

About the Author

Vera Webster is widely recognized in the publishing field as an editor and author of science and environmental materials for both the juvenile and adult readers. She has conducted numerous educational seminars and workshops to provide teachers and parents with opportunities to learn more about children and their learning process. A North Carolina resident and mother of two grown daughters, Mrs. Webster is the president of Creative Resource Systems, Inc.